THE NEW CREEPY CRAWLY COLLECTION

BUTTERFLIES

For a free color catalog describing Gareth Stevens' list of high-quality books and multimedia programs, call 1-800-542-2595 (USA) or 1-800-461-9120 (Canada). Gareth Stevens Publishing's Fax: (414) 225-0377. See our catalog, too, on the World Wide Web: http://gsinc.com

Library of Congress Cataloging-in-Publication Data

Coleman, Graham, 1963-
    Butterflies / by Graham Coleman ; illustrated by Tony Gibbons.
      p. cm. -- (The New creepy crawly collection)
    Includes bibliographical references and index.
    Summary: Examines the anatomy, behavior, life cycle, and legends
of butterflies.
    ISBN 0-8368-1911-X (lib. bdg.)
    1. Butterflies--Juvenile literature. [1. Butterflies.] I. Gibbons, Tony, ill.
II. Title. III. Series.
QL544.2.C65 1997
595.78'9--dc21   97-7343

This North American edition first published in 1997 by
Gareth Stevens Publishing
1555 North RiverCenter Drive, Suite 201
Milwaukee, Wisconsin 53212 USA

This U.S. edition © 1997 by Gareth Stevens, Inc. Created with original © 1996 by Quartz Editorial Services, 112 Station Road, Edgware HA8 7AQ U.K.

Additional illustrations by Clare Heronneau.

Consultant: Matthew Robertson, Senior Keeper, Bristol Zoo, Bristol, England.

Printed in Mexico

1 2 3 4 5 6 7 8 9 01 00 99 98 97

BUTTERFLIES

by Graham Coleman
Illustrated by Tony Gibbons

Gareth Stevens Publishing
MILWAUKEE

Contents

Getting to know
butterflies

Butterflies are some of the most beautiful and enchanting of all creatures in the insect world. In fact, they are so attractive it is hard to believe they start their lives as prickly, creepy-crawly caterpillars. Only later do they change into the colorful flying creatures we know and love.

There are about 18,000 different types of butterflies in the world, and experts are always discovering new species. Some, however, are becoming rare.

How far can butterflies travel? How can you attract them to a garden? Is it right to collect butterflies? Are they helpful creatures or nasty pests? Is it true they can taste with their feet? How are they born? Are any of them poisonous?

Look through this book and discover the fascinating world of the butterfly. On pages 6-7, you can see the largest known butterfly, the Queen Alexandra's birdwing from New Guinea, at about its actual size.

5

Beautiful

Butterflies (and their close relatives, the moths) belong to a group of insects scientists call *Lepidoptera* (LEP-EE-DOP-TUH-RA), a name that means "scaly wings."

A butterfly's wings are not only lovely but much stronger than they look. They can carry their owner across an entire continent during migration. Some butterflies also have wings with blood that contains a special chemical to keep them from freezing if they encounter icy weather.

Let's now examine the rest of the butterfly's body. Like the bodies of other insects, it has three main sections — the head, the thorax, and the abdomen.

Three pairs of legs, each of which is divided into four parts, are attached to the thorax. But the first pair of legs is sometimes very weak and kept tucked up under the butterfly's head.

creatures

A butterfly can see quite well, but its eyes are not nearly as useful as its antennae. These powerful sensors stick out from its head and can pick up scents over great distances through thousands of tiny holes that act as sophisticated smelling devices. Butterflies use their antennae to find both mates and food and often clean them so they remain in good working order.

Once it rests on a flower, a butterfly might start feeding on the sweet substance called nectar. To do this, it unrolls its long, tongue-like sucking tube known as a proboscis. The proboscis can reach far down into the flower's stem where the nectar is kept.

Amazingly, a butterfly does not rely on a tongue but can use its feet to "taste" leaves! Just by feeling the surface of a leaf with its feet, the butterfly can tell if it is the right type of leaf on which to lay eggs.

Magnificent

▼ Let's take a look at four of the world's enormous variety of butterflies. First of all, meet the Monarch, *below*, a North American migrating butterfly. Its markings occur on both sides of the wings and look pretty, but birds need to beware — Monarch caterpillars and the butterfly itself are very poisonous!

▲ The long-tailed Figtree butterfly, *above*, can be found in most parts of Africa. Just look at those stunning blue patches on the reddish wings! The undersides of the wings, however, are a plain orange-brown color.

8

markings

▼ The Cairns birdwing, *below*, is from Southeast Asia and northern Australia. The flashes of red on the green wings show it is a male. The females are quite different. Their basic coloring is black with white markings on the wings.

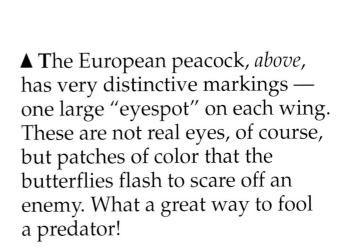

▲ The European peacock, *above*, has very distinctive markings — one large "eyespot" on each wing. These are not real eyes, of course, but patches of color that the butterflies flash to scare off an enemy. What a great way to fool a predator!

Creating a butterfly garden

If you are lucky enough to have a garden, but butterflies do not seem to visit it very often, you might like to try some ways of attracting them.

A first step is to make sure the garden will appeal to female butterflies that are looking for a place to lay their eggs. Butterflies like to lay their eggs on certain plants — nettles, thistles, and clover seem to be particular favorites. Plant some in a sunny corner of your garden and, in summer, you can watch for some colorful visitors.

Butterflies also like to feed on the nectar in the flowers of particular plants. In fact, the buddleia in this picture is often called the "butterfly bush" because they love its nectar and are attracted to it.

But even if you do not have a garden, you might like to study caterpillars that will become butterflies as described on pages 14-17. You can keep your caterpillars in plastic boxes with air holes. Do not put too many in one box. If you find they are cannibalistic and eat each other, keep them individually.

Each day, supply your caterpillars with fresh plant food. Line the box with blotting paper so it is easy to clean. As the caterpillars grow, they will need larger boxes and twigs on which to pupate. Once at the pupa stage, however, they no longer need food. When a butterfly emerges and its wings have dried out, it can be released at the spot where you found the original caterpillar to fly free at last.

11

Butterflies have the most wonderful wings. They reflect sunlight and give butterflies their remarkable coloring. The wing you can see here is from a Chinese red lacewing butterfly.

The patterns and colors on a butterfly's wings are useful, too, because they send out messages. They can be used to attract mates or to warn off enemies, such as birds or lizards.

Butterflies have two sets of wings, with the front set overlapping the smaller back wings. Before it has enough energy to fly, a butterfly has to warm up. It does this by sitting in the sunlight or by shaking its wings to prepare the muscles that control its flight.

wing

Due to its small size, a butterfly may appear to fly fast because of the way it flutters its wings as it moves. Most often it will reach a speed of little more than 6-9 miles (10-15 kilometers) per hour — about a human's jogging pace.

However, if danger approaches, butterflies can dash away, flapping their wings up to six hundred times a minute. Sometimes, though, butterflies flap their wings just once and then rely on wind currents to float them along.

Every time a butterfly flaps its wings, many of the tiny colored scales fall off in the wind. Sunlight also has the effect of fading the brightness of the wing scales. So, as a butterfly grows old, its wings tend to get paler. This means that by the time a red lacewing nears the end of its short life span, its wings will no longer be as highly colored as the one in this illustration.

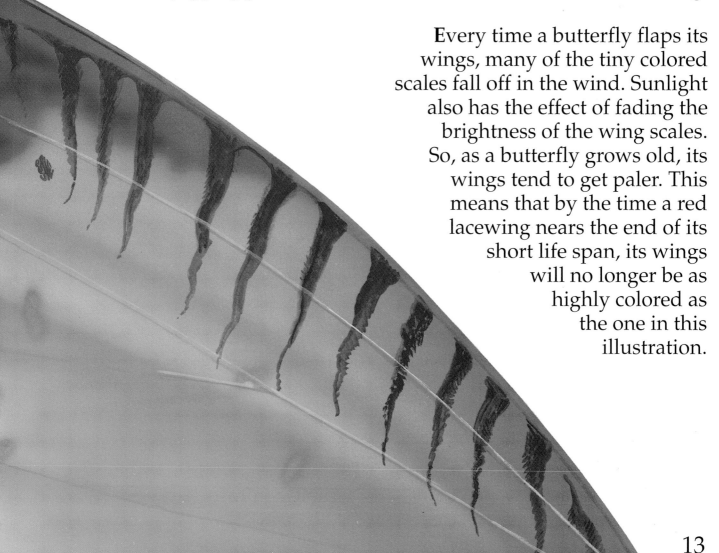

13

Birth of a

When you were born, you looked just like a smaller version of the young person you are today.

Before they become adults, butterflies go through several stages and look different during each, as you can see in this sequence of pictures.

But that's not true for any butterfly species.

The birth of a butterfly is a fascinating process.

butterfly

After mating with a male, the female lays her eggs. You can see them on a leaf, *opposite*. There may be just two or three, or many more; the number varies from one type of butterfly to another.

Two or three weeks later, larvae hatch (*below, left*) and eat the eggshells.

Then the female abandons her eggs.

These then become the caterpillars you can see *above*. They still look nothing at all like the butterflies they eventually become.

15

Butterfly

Something extraordinary happens after the caterpillar has molted four or five times. First the caterpillar finds a quiet place, well away from enemies. Sometimes this may mean hiding in a tree, hollowing out a space for itself under the ground, or resting on a leaf.

Suddenly the caterpillar's skin begins to split. The skin falls off to reveal a pupa, or chrysalis (*below*). The pupa does not move around like a caterpillar but remains still. The pupae of some butterflies are shaped like twigs or leaves. This makes them hard to spot, and they have a better chance of survival.

A new stage is now about to begin.

metamorphosis

After a couple of weeks, or even a few months, the pupa splits so the adult can free itself. The legs and antennae come out first, before the body.

Metamorphosis is now complete.

Then the butterfly stretches its crumpled wings and flies off.

Save the

The rarest and largest butterfly of all is probably the Queen Alexandra's birdwing. It lives in only one part of Papua New Guinea and became rare as the rain forest was cleared for farming. With a wingspan of 12 inches (30 cm), the Queen Alexandra's birdwing is now listed as an endangered species and protected by international law. Sadly, several other types of butterflies are also at risk or have even disappeared altogether. Among them is the Large Blue, which was native to Great Britain and is probably extinct by now. This happened because its caterpillars once fed on the grubs and eggs of red ants. But these ants stopped nesting in the grass, which either became overgrown or turned over by farmers for their crops. How pretty these butterflies must have been as they brightened up Britain's grassy hillsides!

butterfly!

Some butterfly collectors pay a lot of money for rare specimens. In 1966, for example, one butterfly sold for $1,785.00. But isn't there something we can do to stop collectors from catching these beautiful creatures, and instead allow the butterflies to survive in all their many varieties? Conservationists who work to save the world's plant and animal life believe we could save many butterfly species by looking after their natural habitats. They also suggest that special butterfly reserves should be set up in various parts of the world where they could thrive, just as larger creatures do in wildlife parks. These would be very colorful places to visit. And what a wonderful way to ensure that future generations of these exquisite creatures continue to brighten up our planet!

Myths and

A wealth of folklore has developed about butterflies — probably because they are such beautiful creatures and humans like to think they are symbolic in some way. One belief, for instance, is that butterflies are responsible for our dreams. Some American Indians believe that if you tie a picture of a butterfly to the bedpost at night you will be sure to have sweet dreams, with no risk of nightmares.

Depending on the color of the first butterfly you see in the morning, some say you will either have a very good or a very bad day. Red, for example, is supposed to be a lucky color. But sometimes you need to see both sides of the wings because the top and bottom surfaces can vary quite a bit in color and design, as in this Gulf fritillary butterfly.

legends

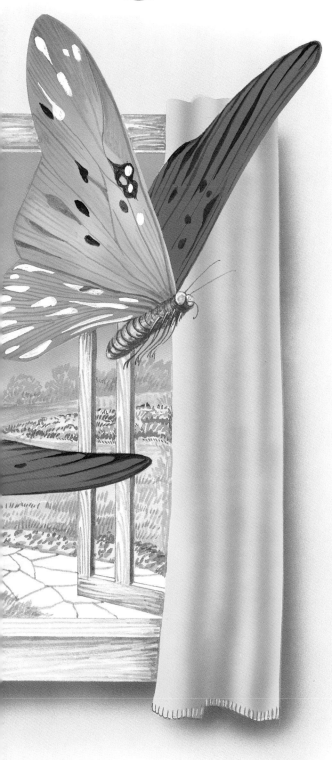

A butterfly that flies into your face is said to predict rain; a white butterfly is a sign of good weather.

If a butterfly comes into your home, there will be a wedding in the family soon. And, according to another piece of folklore, our souls become butterflies when we die and then wing their way to heaven.

We also use phrases about butterflies in everyday speech. A butterfly kiss happens if your eyelashes lightly stroke the cheek of the person you are kissing. And someone is said to be butterfly-like if he or she constantly flits from one thing to another, unable to concentrate.

Of course, there is little to show that any of these stories are more than legends. But it is interesting that humans have woven so many myths around the butterfly.

Did you know?

▼ **What is the difference between a butterfly and a moth?**
Moths are usually much duller in color than butterflies, as you can see from the moth *below*. The antennae of a butterfly always end in a bump, but a moth's antennae do not have bumps. Moths usually fly at night and butterflies during the day. When resting, moths hold their wings flat against their bodies, while butterflies hold theirs straight up.

Is it true that some caterpillars eat and drink strange things?
Some caterpillars have odd appetites. They will eat the larvae of ants, carcasses of dead creatures, or even animal excrement (droppings). The caterpillars of some butterflies are cannibals and may eat each other.

How can you tell a male butterfly from a female?
They may be a different size or have different markings. The male orange tip, for instance, has orange tips on its wings, just as its name suggests; but the female has no orange coloration at all. Sometimes it is very difficult to tell the difference even if you are an expert.

Do butterflies smell?
Some, such as the Apollo, give off a bad smell when danger threatens. Most butterflies have special scent patches that they use to sniff each other out with their antennae prior to mating.

Do butterflies migrate?

Some butterflies travel a very long way at certain times of the year in search of food or more suitable weather. The Monarch butterfly, for example, leaves its breeding sites in Canada and the northern United States to winter in Mexico, traveling a distance of some 1,870 miles (over 3,000 km).

What kind of habitat do butterflies search for?

You can find butterflies all over the world — in meadows, heathlands, bogs, marshes, woodlands, or even in mountains. You would rarely find them in freezing conditions or in the middle of the day in scorching desert areas.

Do butterflies have enemies?

Many insects prey on butterfly larvae. Other creatures, too, such as frogs, spiders, lizards, and birds prey on butterflies. In some remote parts of the world, the larvae of certain butterflies are hunted and cooked by humans and are considered a great delicacy. But please do not try to eat them; some butterfly species can be very poisonous!

▲ How do some butterflies camouflage themselves?

In flight, even the so-called "dead-leaf" butterflies are brightly colored. But when they close their wings, they look just like foliage. This is an excellent form of camouflage, as this butterfly, from India, shown *above* in flight and at rest on a tree, clearly demonstrates.

Glossary

antennae — movable sensory organs, or feelers, on the head of an insect that are used for touching and smelling.

cannibals — organisms that feed on others of their own kind.

habitat — the natural home of a plant or animal.

larva — the wingless stage of an insect's life cycle between egg and pupa.

mate (v) — to join (animals) together to produce young.

metamorphosis — a change in form or appearance that usually occurs in several stages.

migration — to move from one place or climate to another, usually on a seasonal basis.

predators — animals that hunt and kill other animals for food.

pupa — the stage of an insect's life between larva and adult.

species — animals or plants that are closely related and often similar in behavior or appearance. Members of the same species can breed together.

thorax — an insect's middle section, or chest cavity, which holds the heart and lungs.

Books and Videos

Butterflies: Magical Metamorphosis. Secrets of the Animal World series. Eulalia García (Gareth Stevens)

Butterflies and Moths. John Feltwell (Dorling Kindersley)

Butterfly Magic for Kids. E. Jaediker Norsgaard (Gareth Stevens)

The Butterfly in the Garden. Animal Habitats series. Paul and Mary Whalley (Gareth Stevens)

Flying Insects. WINGS series. Patricia Lantier-Sampon (Gareth Stevens)

Butterflies. (Pyramid Film and Video)

Butterflies Are. (Barr Films)

Index

24